AF255475

The **Ultimate**

30-Day Whole Foods

Cookbook for Beginners

1000 Days Quickly & Healthy Recipes and 4-Week Meal Plan to Help You Start Whole Foods

Claudia Broyles

Table of Contents

Introduction **5**

What is the 30 Days Whole Foods Diet? 5

How to Follow the 30 Days Whole Foods Diet 6

Benefits of the 30 Days Whole Foods Diet 6

Foods Allowed on the 30 Days Whole Foods Diet........ 6

Restricted Foods on the 30 Days Whole Foods Diet 7

How Can the 30 Days Whole Foods Diet Work for You?

.... 7

Breakfast Recipes **8**

Healthy Eggs Benedict 8

Egg Muffins 10

Sweet Potato Hash 11

Pork Breakfast Salad 12

Banana Smoothie Bowl....................................... 13

Zucchini Noodles Breakfast 14

Pumpkin and Almond Porridge............................. 15

Super Quick Breakfast Skillet.............................. 16

Berry Smoothie 17

Chorizo Omelet.. 18

Moroccan Omelet.. 19

Waffle Omelet 20

Spinach Coconut Smoothie.................................. 21

Lunch Recipes **22**

Potato Pork Salad.. 22

Stuffed Sweet Potatoes 23

Cauliflower Rice Curry 24

Shakshuka Delight... 25

Chicken Fajitas 26

Parsnip Alfredo 27

Carnitas Delight.. 28

Lamb Stew 29

Egg Salad 30

Potato Chili 31

Pineapple Chicken... 32

Asparagus Delight 33

Chicken Wings... 34

Chicken Broccoli Stir Fry 35

Cauliflower Mash 36

Chicken Salad 37

Lime Coconut Chicken 38

Dinner Recipes **39**

Chicken Pie Soup.. 39

Thai Chicken Coconut Soup 40

Chicken Soup 41

Healthy Toscana Soup.. 42

Tomato Soup.. 43

Broccoli Soup 44

Buffalo Chicken Chowder 45

Cauliflower Rice Chicken Curry 46

Ginger Carrot Soup 47

Stuffed Pepper Soup 48

Lemon Pepper Salmon 49

Broccoli Salad 50

Roast Beef 51

Butternut Squash Hash 52

Brussels Sprouts Chicken Skillet 53

Lemon Chicken 54

Pepper Chicken 55

Veggies with Sausages 56

Chicken with Avocado Salad 57

Salmon Veg Salad 58

Snacks and Sides Recipes 59

Roasted Radish 59

Roast Potatoes 60

Roasted Cauliflower 61

Thyme Roasted Carrots 62

Brussels Sprouts 63

Green Beans with Roasted Almonds 64

Green Beans with Garlic 65

Roasted Red Cabbage 66

Mash Potatoes 67

Cilantro Cauliflower Rice 68

Dessert Recipes 69

Strawberry Ice Cream 69

Chia Coconut Pudding 70

Mango Banana Ice Cream 71

Strawberry Coconut Cream 72

Sweet Fruit Salad 73

Avocado Ice Cream 74

Coconut Chocolate Pudding 75

Caramel Apples 76

Blueberry Delight 77

Avocado Mousse 78

Basic Dressings, Sauces, and Condiments Recipes 79

Balsamic Salad Dressing 79

Sesame Dressing 80

Burger Sauce 81

Lemon Dressing 82

Ranch Dressing 83

Cashew Curry Dip 84

Cheesy Buffalo Sauce 85

Avocado Dip 86

Chimichurri Sauce 87

Buffalo Dill Sauce 88

30 Days Meal Plan 89

Conclusion 92

Introduction

The term "whole foods" generally refers to any food that is predominantly in its natural state. Whole foods do not contain any added sugars, flavors, starches, or artificial ingredients. As they are usually not produced in a factory, they can be described as the exact opposite of processed foods. Whole foods are not as addictive as foods that have added sugar. Undoubtedly, a diet dominated by natural, unrefined, unprocessed whole foods is a healthy and nutritious one. It is rich in minerals, fiber, vitamins, and other essential nutrients and ingredients.

What is the 30 Days Whole Foods Diet?

Generally speaking, a whole foods diet is not a specific eating habit or regimen dictated by nutritional experts or books. Instead, it can simply be classified as eating a natural and clean diet entirely free from any processed food.

The 30 Days Whole Foods Diet, however, does set out a particular eating plan. It restricts legumes, dairy, alcohol, grains, and additives from your diet plan. It is a month-long, healthy and nutritious diet plan, introduced in 2009 by two certified nutritionists to boost metabolism and promote healthy eating. The diet is primarily based on the idea that certain food groups can be harmful to the overall health of your body.

How to Follow the 30 Days Whole Foods Diet

The concept behind the 30 Days Whole Foods Diet is very simple. You simply remove those foods from your eating list that may potentially harm or negatively impact your health. However, the diet has a strict set of rules that it's important to follow carefully. These rules are as follows:

• There is a list of allowed and restricted foods. This list needs to be strictly adhered to and without any cheating.

• If you get off-track from your diet (e.g., eat a forbidden food), you have to start again from day one.

• Unlike other diets, there is no need to count or track calories, points, or portion sizes. Plus, you only need to weigh yourself on the first and last day (30th day) of your diet.

• Smoking is strictly prohibited while following the diet.

Benefits of the 30 Days Whole Foods Diet

Following the 30 Days Whole Foods Diet, you should lose weight and start to enjoy various health benefits. Some of the ways in which the diet boosts your overall well-being include:

• It promotes fat loss, increased energy levels, lowered food cravings, improved physical stamina, and also promotes better and sound sleep.

• The diet also promotes healthy eating as a lifestyle and changes the general narrative about food.

• The strict restriction of certain foods allows your body to reset itself to its natural state free from any gut disruptions, hormonal imbalances, or inflammation caused by certain food categories.

Foods Allowed on the 30 Days Whole Foods Diet

The foods allowed on the 30 Days Whole Foods Diet are strictly unprocessed. The diet also promotes the habit of choosing foods with the shortest ingredient list or only with ingredients that you recognize. Foods allowed are:

1. **Fish & seafood** like shrimp, calamari, lobster, scallops, anchovies, crab, fish, etc.

2. **Meat & poultry**, such as veal, duck, beef, turkey, lamb, pork, chicken, etc.

3. **Eggs** of all kinds, including foods made from eggs like homemade mayo.

4. All types of **veggies**.

5. Both **dried and fresh fruits**. However, fresh fruits are preferred.

6. **Fats** like coconut oil, clarified butter, healthy plant oils, ghee, and duck fat.

7. Nuts & seeds of all kinds apart from peanuts which are classified as legumes. Moreover, flour, milk, and butter made from nuts are also allowed on the 30 Days Whole Foods Diet.

Restricted Foods on the 30 Days Whole Foods Diet

The following foods are considered a strict no-no while following the 30 Days Whole Foods Diet.

1. Alcoholic beverages of all kinds, including spirits, wines, beer, and liqueurs.

2. All kinds of **grains**, irrespective of whether or not they are processed, including corn, rice, oats, and wheat.

3. Artificial sweeteners and sugar like honey, agave syrup, raw sugar, maple syrup, and all products that contain these ingredients or any kind of artificial sweeteners are restricted.

4. Dairy products like sheep, goat, and cow's milk, cheese, ice cream, yogurt, and other similar products from dairy are restricted. Only clarified ghee or butter is allowed.

5. Legumes and pulses like beans, lentils, peas, and even peanut butter are restricted. However, sugar snap peas, snow peas, and green beans are allowed.

6. Processed additives, such as MSG, carrageenan, sulfites, or foods containing these ingredients are strictly prohibited.

7. Soy products like edamame, tempeh, tofu, and all products derived from soy, like soy sauce or miso, are also restricted.

8. The **baking of certain foods, snacks, and treats** is also restricted on the diet. You are not allowed to have foods like paleo pancakes or cauliflower pizza crust.

The concept of cheat meals is also not a part of the 30 Days Whole Foods Diet. Instead, the diet promotes adhering strictly to the allowed and restricted food lists and remaining on track. Any slippage from the diet means that you have to start again from day one.

How Can the 30 Days Whole Foods Diet Work for You?

A calorie deficit promotes weight loss, and the 30 Days Whole Foods Diet helps you achieve this because of its restrictive nature. However, the 30 Days Whole Foods Diet is a lifestyle and not a short-term diet regime. To maintain the weight loss, you need to continue it for the long term. Or else, any progress will be lost, and you'll find the weight being put back on. You must be willing to commit to sticking to the guidelines and rules regarding allowed and restricted foods. The Whole Foods diet is not a quick fix; it means being ready to make permanent changes to your eating habits and how you look at the food you are putting in your body.

Healthy Eggs Benedict

Preparation Time: 30 minutes
Cooking Time: 10 minutes
Servings: 4

Ingredients:

- 1 sweet potato (cut into ½ inch round slices)
- 4 eggs
- 4 slices bacon
- Parsley (for garnish)

For sauce:

- 3 egg yolks
- 1 tablespoon lemon juice
- ½ teaspoon Dijon mustard
- ¼ teaspoon salt
- ½ cup butter (hot)
- Pinch of cayenne pepper

Preparation:

1. Preheat the oven to 400°F.
2. Slice the sweet potato into ½ inch round slices.
3. Place the slices of sweet potato on a baking dish and bake for 30 minutes.
4. While the sweet potatoes are baking, take a large pan and place it on medium heat. Cook the bacon in the pan for 1 minute on each side. Set aside.
5. To prepare the eggs, take a pot of water and bring it to a simmer. Crack the eggs into the water and poach them in the simmering water for 4 minutes.
6. Place the cooked eggs aside in a separate bowl.
7. In a blender, add the egg yolks, Dijon mustard, lemon juice, and cayenne pepper. Blend for 5 to 10 seconds.
8. Pour the hot butter into the blender slowly.
9. Blend until all the ingredients are combined and then pour into another bowl.
10. Once the sweet potatoes are baked, layer them with the bacon and poached eggs, and drizzle over the sauce.

Serving Suggestion: You can use chopped parsley to sprinkle over the sauce.

Variation Tip: You can use chopped chives instead of parsley for the garnish or use them together for extra depth of flavor.

Nutritional Information per Serving:

Calories: 370| **Fat:** 33g| **Sat Fat:** 18g| **Carbohydrates:** 5g| **Fiber:** 1g| **Sugar:** 1g| **Protein:** 14g

Egg Muffins

Preparation Time: 15 minutes
Cooking Time: 25 minutes
Servings: 12

Ingredients:

- 12 eggs
- Salt to taste
- Pepper to taste
- 4 cups broccoli florets
- 3 slices bacon (½ inch thick pieces)
- 1½ teaspoons nutritional yeast
- ½ cup chives (finely sliced)

Preparation:

1. Preheat the oven to 350°F.
2. Take a large bowl and crack the eggs into it.
3. Season the eggs with salt and pepper.
4. Whisk the eggs until they become fluffy.
5. Take a large pan and place it on medium heat. Add the bacon slices and cook until they become crispy, and put them on a plate.
6. Take a pot half-filled with water and bring it to the boil.
7. Insert a steamer basket into the pot and add the broccoli to it. Cover with the lid and cook for 6 minutes.
8. Open the lid, remove the steamer from the pot, and set the broccoli florets aside until they have cooled slightly.
9. Dice the broccoli into tiny pieces.
10. Add the bacon, broccoli, and nutritional yeast into the egg mixture.
11. Pour the mixture into a muffin tray and bake for 25 minutes.

Serving Suggestion: Serve warm with the chopped chives on top.

Variation Tip: You can add some dried herbs to the egg mix to enhance the taste of the muffins.

Nutritional Information per Serving:

Calories: 112| **Fat:** 7.6g|**Sat Fat:** 3.4g|**Carbohydrates:** 2.6g|**Fiber:** 0.8g|**Sugar:** 1g|**Protein:** 8.8g

Sweet Potato Hash

Preparation Time: 15 minutes
Cooking Time: 20 minutes
Servings: 4

Ingredients:

- 4 slices bacon (½ inch thick pieces)
- 1 onion, diced
- 1 red bell pepper, diced
- 1 sweet potato, peeled and diced
- 2 cups kale leaves, chopped
- ½ teaspoon cumin
- ¼ teaspoon garlic powder
- ¼ teaspoon paprika
- Salt to taste
- Pepper to taste
- 1 scallion onion, sliced
- 4 eggs

Preparation:

1. Take a large pan and place it on medium heat.
2. Add the bacon and sauté until crispy and golden.
3. Remove the bacon and put it into a small bowl.
4. Add the red bell pepper and onion and sauté for 1 minute.
5. Add the sweet potato into the pan and cook for 10 minutes, stirring continuously.
6. Put a lid on the pan and cook for 5 minutes to soften the potatoes.
7. Remove the lid and add the kale and bacon into the pan and cook for 1 minute.
8. Take a spatula and create four wells into the mixture in the pan.   Crack the eggs into the wells one by one.
9. Cook until the eggs are done as you prefer.
10. Season the sweet potato hash with the scallion, salt, and pepper.

Serving Suggestion: If you prefer, skip the eggs, and add avocado instead.

Variation Tip: Sprinkle some nutritional yeast on top for an enhanced flavor.

Nutritional Information per Serving:

Calories: 222| **Fat:** 13g|**Sat Fat:** 4g|**Carbohydrates:** 15g|**Fiber:** 2g|**Sugar:** 4g|**Protein:** 11g

Pork Breakfast Salad

Preparation Time: 20 minutes
Cooking Time: 20 minutes
Servings: 5

Ingredients:

- 1 pound pork, minced
- 9 eggs, boiled
- 3 cups cherry tomatoes, halved
- ¼ cup onion, thinly sliced
- 2 avocados, diced
- ½ cup fresh cilantro or parsley, chopped
- Salt to taste
- ¼ teaspoon black pepper
- ¼ cup lemon juice

Preparation:

1. Preheat the oven to 400°F.
2. Take a baking sheet and place parchment paper over it.
3. Make meatballs out of the minced pork and bake for 15 minutes or until they are cooked.
4. Set them aside.
5. Peel the eggs and slice them into eight pieces.
6. Take a bowl and add all the remaining ingredients, including the meatballs.
7. Stir well until the eggs and avocado become a bit creamy.
8. You can top the dish off with fresh herbs of your choice.

Serving Suggestion: Top with a drizzle of olive oil before serving.

Variation Tip: You can use bacon or sausages instead of pork.

Nutritional Information per Serving:

Calories: 489| **Fat:** 35.6g|**Sat Fat:** 9g|**Carbohydrates:** 11.6g|**Fiber:** 5.2g|**Sugar:** 4.1g|**Protein:** 31.5g

Banana Smoothie Bowl

Preparation Time: 5 minutes
Cooking Time: 0 minutes
Servings: 1

Ingredients:

- 1 banana, frozen
- 1 cup frozen cherries
- 1 tablespoon almond butter
- 1 tablespoon unsweetened coconut flakes
- ½ cup almond milk
- 2 teaspoons maca powder

For toppings:

- ½ cup cherries
- Any nuts that you like (walnuts, cashews, almonds, etc.)

Preparation:

1. Take a blender and add all ingredients except for the ingredients for topping.
2. Blend until a smooth paste is produced.
3. Pour it out into a bowl.
4. Add the toppings and enjoy!

Serving Suggestion: Add some sliced strawberries on top.

Variation Tip: Instead of cherries, use any type of berries you prefer.

Nutritional Information per Serving:

Calories: 602| **Fat:** 39.1g|**Sat Fat:** 26.7g|**Carbohydrates:** 64.9g|**Fiber:** 10.3g|**Sugar:** 33.3g|**Protein:** 9.3g

Zucchini Noodles Breakfast

Preparation Time: 15 minutes
Cooking Time: 15 minutes
Servings: 2

Ingredients:

- 1 large zucchini, spiralized
- ½ avocado
- ¼ cup olive oil
- 2 tablespoons water
- 2 garlic cloves, peeled
- 2 sweet potatoes, peeled and diced
- 2 eggs, poached
- 2 tablespoons chopped scallions for garnish
- Salt to taste
- Pepper to taste

Preparation:

1. Take a large skillet and place it on medium heat.
2. Add 2 tablespoons of olive oil.
3. Add the sweet potatoes and cook, stirring often.
4. Once the potatoes are cooked, set them aside.
5. In the same skillet, add the zucchini noodles and cook for 3 minutes until they are warm.
6. Bring a pan of water to a simmer, crack in the eggs, and poach until done.
7. In a blender, add the avocado, garlic, 2 tablespoons of olive oil, the water, and blend to make the avocado cream.
8. Add the avocado cream to the same skillet the noodles were in.
9. Add the potatoes and stir well.
10. Place on a serving dish and serve with the eggs.

Serving Suggestion: Add fresh chilies or Italian seasoning for extra flavor.

Variation Tip: Use fried eggs instead of poached.

Nutritional Information per Serving:

Calories: 544| **Fat:** 39g|**Sat Fat:** 6g|**Carbohydrates:** 57g|**Fiber:** 12g|**Sugar:** 15g|**Protein:** 13g

Pumpkin and Almond Porridge

Preparation Time: 5 minutes
Cooking Time: 15 minutes
Servings: 1

Ingredients:

- 1 cup canned pumpkin
- ⅓ cup almond pulp
- 1 tablespoon chia seeds
- ⅓ cup almond milk
- Pinch sea salt
- ½ teaspoon ground cinnamon

Preparation:

1. Take a large saucepan and place on medium heat.
2. Add the almond pulp, chia seeds, pumpkin, milk, sea salt, and cinnamon to the pan.
3. Stir until the mixture starts to boil.
4. Let the porridge mixture simmer for 5 to 10 minutes.
5. Top with toppings of your choice and serve.

Serving Suggestion: Add a few dates or other dried fruits on top before serving.

Variation Tip: You can use any nut milk you prefer.

Nutritional Information per Serving:

Calories: 310| **Fat:** 20.1g|**Sat Fat:** 17.3g|**Carbohydrates:** 34.5g|**Fiber:** 9.8g|**Sugar:** 18.7g|**Protein:** 4.8g

Super Quick Breakfast Skillet

Preparation Time: 2 minutes
Cooking Time: 15 minutes
Servings: 4

Ingredients:

- 1 teaspoon oil
- 1 pound ground beef
- 1 cup salsa
- 6 eggs

Preparation:

1. Take a skillet, add oil and place it over medium heat.
2. Once the skillet is hot, add the beef and cook for 8 to 10 minutes until it is no longer pink. Stir occasionally.
3. Add the salsa mixture and cook for 3 more minutes.
4. Crack the eggs into the skillet and cook to your own preference.
5. Serve hot.

Serving Suggestion: You can use fried, poached, or scrambled eggs.

Variation Tip: Add any of your favorite veggies to the dish.

Nutritional Information per Serving:

Calories: 556| **Fat:** 32g|**Sat Fat:** 7.2g|**Carbohydrates:** 9.2g|**Fiber:** 2.1g|**Sugar:** 5g|**Protein:** 65.2g

Berry Smoothie

Preparation Time: 3 minutes
Cooking Time: 0 minutes
Servings: 2

Ingredients:

- ¼ cup strawberries
- ¼ cup blackberries
- ¼ cup cranberries
- ¼ cup blueberries
- 1 cup spinach
- 1 banana
- 1 tablespoon chia seeds
- 1 tablespoon hemp hearts
- 1 teaspoon ground flax seed
- ½ cup coconut milk
- ½ cup water
- 5 mint leaves

Preparation:

1. Take a blender, add all the ingredients, and blend.
2. Blend until the smoothie has reached the desired consistency.
3. Serve and enjoy!

Serving Suggestion: Serve with chia seeds on top.

Variation Tip: You can add kale or chard instead of spinach.

Nutritional Information per Serving:

Calories: 287| **Fat:** 18.6g|**Sat Fat:** 13.2g|**Carbohydrates:** 29.5g|**Fiber:** 9.2g|**Sugar:** 12.9g|**Protein:** 7g

Chorizo Omelet

Preparation Time: 5 minutes
Cooking Time: 20 minutes
Servings: 2

Ingredients:

- 5 teaspoons coconut oil
- ¼ cup onion, diced
- 1 garlic clove, minced
- 1 green bell pepper, diced
- ¼ pound chorizo, removed from casing
- 4 eggs
- 2 tablespoons coconut milk
- ¼ teaspoon sea salt
- ⅛ teaspoon black pepper

Preparation:

1. Take a large pan, add the oil, and heat over medium heat.
2. Add the onion and garlic, and sauté for about 3 minutes.
3. Add the bell pepper and cook for one minute.
4. Add in the chorizo and cook for 5 minutes, stirring occasionally. Set aside when cooked.
5. Take a bowl and add the eggs, milk, sea salt, and pepper. Whisk well.
6. Take another round skillet and place it over low heat. Add 1 teaspoon of oil.
7. Pour half of the egg mixture into the skillet and make sure it is spread evenly. Cook the mixture for about 2 minutes.
8. Add half of the chorizo mixture over half of the cooked egg.
9. Fold the egg omelet in half to create a half-circle and place it on a plate.
10. Repeat steps 7 to 9 with the remaining mixture.

Serving Suggestion: Plate up the omelet with avocado slices, salsa, or mayo.

Variation Tip: Adding some cayenne pepper will enhance the flavor of the omelet.

Nutritional Information per Serving:

Calories: 464| **Fat:** 38g|**Sat Fat:** 18g|**Carbohydrates:** 7g|**Fiber:** 1g|**Sugar:** 2g|**Protein:** 20g

Moroccan Omelet

Preparation Time: 5 minutes
Cooking Time: 7 minutes
Servings: 1

Ingredients:

- 1 tablespoon extra-virgin olive oil
- ¾ cup canned tomato sauce
- ½ teaspoon cumin
- 2 tablespoons chopped parsley
- ¼ teaspoon salt
- ¼ teaspoon pepper
- 3 eggs

Preparation:

1. Take a large skillet and place it on medium heat.
2. Add the olive oil and heat it.
3. Once the oil is hot, add the tomato sauce and cook for 1 minute.
4. Add in the parsley, salt, and pepper and let it simmer for 5 minutes.
5. Take a large bowl and whisk the eggs in it.
6. Drizzle the eggs over the tomato mixture in the skillet, ensuring it is evenly distributed.
7. Place a lid on top and cook for 4 to 5 minutes.
8. Once the egg is completely set and cooked, transfer it onto a plate, serve, and enjoy!

Serving Suggestion: Sprinkle some fresh cilantro leaves on top.

Variation Tip: Add some nutritional yeast to the egg mixture before cooking for a flavor enhancement.

Nutritional Information per Serving:

Calories: 364| **Fat:** 21g|**Sat Fat:** 6g|**Carbohydrates:** 10g|**Fiber:** 3g|**Sugar:** 4g|**Protein:** 19g

Waffle Omelet

Preparation Time: 10 minutes
Cooking Time: 8 minutes
Servings: 2

Ingredients:

- 4 eggs
- 1 potato, grated
- ¼ bell pepper, diced
- 2 tablespoons onion, diced
- 1 teaspoon cilantro
- 2 slices chipotle bacon, diced and cooked

Preparation:

1. Take a large bowl and add in every ingredient. Whisk well.
2. Heat the waffle iron at a medium-low setting.
3. Spray some cooking oil on the waffle iron.
4. Add the mixture to the waffle iron, but do not close it.
5. Once the mixture starts to cook, close the iron and cook for 4 minutes.
6. Take out and serve.

Serving Suggestion: Add avocado slices on top for a creamy taste.

Variation Tip: Sprinkle on some chopped jalapeno for a kick of flavor.

Nutritional Information per Serving:

Calories: 411| **Fat:** 25g|**Sat Fat:** 5g|**Carbohydrates:** 31g|**Fiber:** 10g|**Sugar:** 5g|**Protein:** 19g

Spinach Coconut Smoothie

Preparation Time: 5 minutes
Cooking Time: 0 minutes
Servings: 1

Ingredients:

- 1 lemon, peeled
- 3 cups baby spinach, washed
- 2 tablespoons sunflower seeds
- 1 cup coconut milk
- 1 cup water
- 1 scoop vanilla protein powder

Preparation:

1. Take a blender and add all the ingredients.
2. Blend until the desired consistency is reached.
3. Serve and enjoy!

Serving Suggestion: Sprinkle some fresh mint leaves on top.

Variation Tip: You can use chia seeds instead of sunflower seeds.

Nutritional Information per Serving:

Calories: 625| **Fat:** 60.8g|**Sat Fat:** 51.1g|**Carbohydrates:** 23.2g|**Fiber:** 9.4g|**Sugar:** 10g|**Protein:** 10.2g

Potato Pork Salad

Preparation Time: 10 minutes
Cooking Time: 0 minutes
Servings: 3

Ingredients:

- 2 tablespoons olive oil
- ½ lemon juice
- ¼ teaspoon paprika
- Salt to taste
- Pepper to taste
- 3 potatoes, cubed
- 9 pounds pork, cooked
- 1 cucumber, sliced
- ½ avocado
- 3 tablespoons fresh parsley

Preparation:

1. Take a large bowl and add the olive oil, lemon juice, paprika, pepper, potatoes, pork, cucumber, avocado, and parsley.
2. Mix the ingredients well.
3. Toss the salad and heat it in the microwave for 1 minute.

Serving Suggestion: Add a drizzle of Tabasco sauce over the salad.

Variation Tip: Red chili flakes can add a kick of flavor.

Nutritional Information per Serving:

Calories: 467| **Fat:** 25g| **Sat Fat:** 5g| **Carbohydrates:** 39g|**Fiber:** 5g| **Sugar:** 5g| **Protein:** 26g

Stuffed Sweet Potatoes

Preparation Time: 10 minutes
Cooking Time: 0 minutes
Servings: 2

Ingredients:

- 6 pounds pork, cooked and shredded
- 2 cups kale
- 2 sweet potatoes, baked
- ½ avocado

Preparation:

1. Make a deep cut in the middle of the baked potatoes for the filling. Do not cut the potatoes completely.
2. Take a bowl, and add the pork, kale, and avocado.
3. Toss the ingredients together well.
4. Place the filling in the potatoes.
5. Reheat the potatoes in the microwave for 1 minute each.
6. Serve hot.

Serving Suggestion: Top with chopped mint leaves before serving.

Variation Tip: You can use chili sauce to enhance the flavor.

Nutritional Information per Serving:

Calories: 486| **Fat:** 23g| **Sat Fat:** 4g| **Carbohydrates:** 47g|**Fiber:** 11g| **Sugar:** 11g|
Protein: 29g

Cauliflower Rice Curry

Preparation Time: 30 minutes
Cooking Time: 20 minutes
Servings: 4

Ingredients:

- 4 cups cauliflower rice
- 2 tablespoons curry powder
- ½ teaspoon cumin
- ½ teaspoon paprika
- ¼ teaspoon sea salt
- 2 tablespoons olive oil
- ¾ cup red onion, chopped
- 1 teaspoon garlic, minced
- 2 teaspoons avocado oil
- 2 cups carrots, chopped
- 4 cups vegetable broth
- 1 cup almond milk

Preparation:

1. Take a bowl and add the cauliflower rice, curry powder, garlic powder, salt, and cumin.
2. Add 3 tablespoons of oil and toss the mixture well.
3. Add the mixture and the remaining ingredients to a large saucepan.
4. Bring it to a boil, and then let it simmer for 20 minutes.
5. Serve and enjoy.

Serving Suggestion: Add chopped cilantro to the finished dish.

Variation Tip: Putting some red chili flakes into the mixture will give some extra spice.

Nutritional Information per Serving:

Calories: 162| **Fat:** 8g| **Sat Fat:** 1.3g| **Carbohydrates:** 20g|**Fiber:** 9g| **Sugar:** 6g|
Protein: 6g

Shakshuka Delight

Preparation Time: 10 minutes
Cooking Time: 20 minutes
Servings: 6

Ingredients:

- 1 onion, diced
- 1 red bell pepper, diced
- 4 garlic cloves, chopped
- 2 teaspoons paprika
- 1 teaspoon cumin
- 3 tomatoes, peeled
- ¼ teaspoon chili powder
- 6 eggs
- 1 bunch parsley, chopped
- 1 bunch cilantro, chopped
- Salt to taste
- Pepper to taste

Preparation:

1. Take a large pan and place it on medium heat.

2. Add olive oil and heat it for a while.

3. Add the onion, bell pepper, garlic and cook for 5 minutes.

4. Add the remaining spices and cook for about 1 minute.

5. Add in the tomatoes and break them down using a large spoon.

6. Add salt and pepper to taste.

7. Let the sauce simmer for a while.

8. Take a large spoon and make wells in the sauce with it.

9. Crack the eggs into the wells and cook for 8 minutes.

10. Garnish, serve and enjoy!

Serving Suggestion: This dish is fantastic with a green salad on the side.

Variation Tip: Add chili flakes to the tomato mixture for extra flavor.

Nutritional Information per Serving:

Calories: 122| **Fat:** 5.4g| **Sat Fat:** 1.6g| **Carbohydrates:** 9.7g|**Fiber:** 1.9g| **Sugar:** 5.5g|
Protein: 8g

Chicken Fajitas

Preparation Time: 10 minutes
Cooking Time: 16 minutes
Servings: 6

Ingredients:

For the Fajitas

- 3 boneless, skinless chicken breasts, cut into slices
- 1 onion, sliced
- 3 bell peppers, sliced
- 2 tablespoons olive oil
- 1 tablespoon lime juice

For the Seasoning

- 1 tablespoon chili powder
- ½ tablespoon cumin
- ½ teaspoon paprika
- ½ teaspoon oregano
- 1 teaspoon garlic powder

- Salt to taste
- Pepper to taste

Preparation:

1. Take a bowl, add the fajita seasoning ingredients and mix well.

2. Take the chicken slices and sprinkle with the fajita seasoning until all sides are covered.

3. Take a large skillet, pour in the oil, and place on medium heat.

4. Cook the chicken for 8 minutes on both sides.

5. Add in the onion and bell peppers, and sauté for a few minutes.

6. Squeeze over the lime juice and stir everything together.

7. Serve and enjoy!

Serving Suggestion: Serve with tomato salsa on the side.

Variation Tip: Replace the black pepper with cayenne pepper for more spice.

Nutritional Information per Serving:

Calories: 140| **Fat:** 7g| **Sat Fat:** 1g| **Carbohydrates:** 7g|**Fiber:** 2g| **Sugar:** 3g| **Protein:** 14g

Parsnip Alfredo

Preparation Time: 20 minutes
Cooking Time: 20 minutes
Servings: 4

Ingredients:

- 1 recipe vegan alfredo sauce
- 1 boneless, skinless chicken breast
- 2 parsnips, peeled
- 6 broccoli florets, boiled
- Salt to taste
- Pepper to taste

Preparation:

1. Spiralize the parsnips to make noodles and then set them aside.

2. Take a large bowl and season the chicken with salt and pepper.

3. In a large skillet, add 1 tablespoon of oil and place it over medium heat.

4. Add in the chicken and cook for 5 minutes on both sides until cooked.

5. Slice the cooked chicken into pieces.

6. Take a large sauté pan, add two tablespoons of oil and place it on medium heat.

7. Add in parsnip noodles and cook for 3 minutes. Stir occasionally.

8. Add in the vegan alfredo sauce and cooked broccoli, stirring continuously.

9. Serve and enjoy!

Serving Suggestion: Chopped parsley and a sprinkling of nutritional yeast over the dish will make it extra yummy.

Variation Tip: Add chili sauce to enhance the taste of the dish.

Nutritional Information per Serving:

Calories: 740| **Fat:** 39g| **Sat Fat:** 5g| **Carbohydrates:** 65g|**Fiber:** 18g| **Sugar:** 14g| **Protein:** 43g

Carnitas Delight

Preparation Time: 10 minutes
Cooking Time: 8 hours
Servings: 8

Ingredients:

- 4 pounds boneless pork
- 1 tablespoon ground cumin
- 1 tablespoon oregano
- 1 teaspoon chili powder
- 1 teaspoon salt
- 1 onion, diced
- 1 teaspoon black pepper
- 4 garlic cloves, diced
- 1 cup orange juice

Preparation:

1. Take a bowl and add the cumin, black pepper, salt, oregano, and chili powder and mix well.

2. Rub the mixture onto the entire piece of pork.

3. Place the pork into a slow cooker.

4. Add in the garlic, orange juice, and onion and close the lid.

5. Cook for 8 hours on a low setting.

6. Once cooked, take out the pork and place it onto a cutting board.

7. Using two forks, shred the pork.

8. Place the shredded pork onto a serving dish and pour over the juice from the slow cooker.

Serving Suggestion: Avocado slices and tomato salsa go perfectly with this dish.

Variation Tip: For some spice, add cayenne pepper to the pork rub.

Nutritional Information per Serving:

Calories: 227| **Fat:** 9g| **Sat Fat:** 3g| **Carbohydrates:** 5g|**Fiber:** 1g| **Sugar:** 2g| **Protein:** 28g

Lamb Stew

Preparation Time: 15 minutes
Cooking Time: 2 hours
Servings: 6

Ingredients:

- 2½ pounds lamb, cubed
- 4 bacon slices, cut into 1-inch pieces
- 2 onions, cubed
- 2 pounds potatoes, peeled and cubed
- 6 carrots, peeled and cubed
- 1 turnip, peeled and cubed
- 1 teaspoon thyme

- 4 cups vegetable/chicken stock
- Salt to taste
- Pepper to taste

Preparation:

1. Take a large bowl, place the lamb in it, and season with salt and pepper.

2. Heat a Dutch oven (or equivalent) on medium heat.

3. Place in the bacon and cook for 4 minutes until crispy.

4. Increase the heat to medium-high and add the pieces of lamb.

5. Mix well with the bacon and then take the mixture out and place it on a plate.

6. Add the onion to the Dutch oven and cook for 3 minutes.

7. Place the lamb-bacon mix back into the Dutch oven.

8. Add in the thyme and broth and bring to a boil.

9. Reduce the heat to low and let simmer for 1 hour.

10. After an hour, add in the remaining ingredients and cook for another 30 minutes.

11. Remove and serve immediately.

Serving Suggestion: Serve with chopped cilantro on top.

Variation Tip: You can add chili flakes and cayenne pepper to enhance the flavor of the dish.

Nutritional Information per Serving:

Calories: 458| **Fat:** 16g| **Sat Fat:** 5g| **Carbohydrates:** 37g|**Fiber:** 6g| **Sugar:** 6g| **Protein:** 36g

Egg Salad

Preparation Time: 10 minutes
Cooking Time: 10 minutes
Servings: 4

Ingredients:

- 8 eggs, hard-boiled and chopped
- ¼ cup mayonnaise
- 2 tablespoons onion, diced
- 1 tablespoon Dijon mustard
- 1 tablespoon chives, chopped
- 1 tablespoon dill, chopped
- ¼ teaspoon salt
- ¼ teaspoon pepper

Preparation:

1. Take a bowl and add all the ingredients. Mix well.

2. That's it! Serve and enjoy!

Serving Suggestion: Eat this dish with carrot, celery, and cucumber sticks.

Variation Tip: Add white pepper to enhance the taste.

Nutritional Information per Serving:

Calories: 258| **Fat:** 21g| **Sat Fat:** 4g| **Carbohydrates:** 2g|**Fiber:** 1g| **Sugar:** 2g| **Protein:** 14g

Potato Chili

Preparation Time: 10 minutes
Cooking Time: 30 minutes
Servings: 8

Ingredients:

- 1 tablespoon avocado oil
- 1 pound ground beef
- 1 pound ground pork
- 1 onion, diced
- 2 garlic cloves, diced
- 2 bell peppers, diced
- 2 sweet potatoes, peeled and cubed
- 2 teaspoons salt
- ½ teaspoon cumin
- 1 teaspoon onion powder
- 1 teaspoon garlic powder
- 2 tablespoons chili powder
- 1 can of tomatoes, crushed
- 1½ cups beef broth

Preparation:

1. Heat up the Dutch oven (or equivalent) and add oil to it.

2. Add in the beef and pork and sauté until they are cooked through.

3. Add all the other ingredients and cook for 5 minutes.

4. Bring the mixture to a boil and then let it simmer for 20 minutes.

5. Serve and enjoy!

Serving Suggestion: Add chopped jalapenos before serving for some extra spice.

Variation Tip: Coconut oil can be used instead of avocado oil.

Nutritional Information per Serving:

Calories: 370| **Fat:** 26g| **Sat Fat:** 6g| **Carbohydrates:** 13g|**Fiber:** 3g| **Sugar:** 4g| **Protein:** 21g

Pineapple Chicken

Preparation Time: 15 minutes
Cooking Time: 20 minutes
Servings: 6

Ingredients:

- 2 pounds boneless chicken, cubed
- 2 garlic cloves, minced
- 2 tablespoons hot sauce
- ½ cup pineapple juice
- 1 tablespoon ginger, grated
- ½ teaspoon red chili flakes
- 2 tablespoons avocado oil
- 1 onion, cubed
- 2 jalapeno slices
- 1 can pineapple chunks, drained
- 1 tablespoon lemon juice
- 1 teaspoon salt
- 1 red bell pepper, cubed
- 1 green bell pepper, cubed
- 1 tablespoon arrowroot starch
- 1 tablespoon water

Preparation:

1. Take a bowl and add the pineapple juice, lemon juice, garlic, hot sauce, ginger, and pepper flakes. Mix well.

2. Take a separate bowl, put in the chicken, and season with salt and pepper.

3. Take a large skillet, add the oil, and heat it over medium heat.

4. Add the chicken and cook for 5 minutes until cooked through.

5. Reduce the heat a little and add more oil.

6. Add in the bell peppers, jalapeno, and onion, and sauté for 3 minutes.

7. Add in all the remaining ingredients along with the pineapple sauce and cook for 3 minutes.

8. Bring the sauce to a boil and then simmer until the preferred thickness is reached.

9. Serve while hot.

Serving Suggestion: Cauliflower rice is the perfect accompaniment to this dish.

Variation Tip: Olive oil can also be used instead of avocado oil.

Nutritional Information per Serving:

Calories: 414| **Fat:** 30g| **Sat Fat:** 7g| **Carbohydrates:** 16g|**Fiber:** 2g| **Sugar:** 4g| **Protein:** 25g

Asparagus Delight

Preparation Time: 5 minutes
Cooking Time: 8 minutes
Servings: 4

Ingredients:

- 1 pound asparagus, trimmed
- Avocado oil spray
- ¼ teaspoon salt
- ⅛ teaspoon pepper

Preparation:

1. Preheat an air-fryer to 390°F.

2. Place the asparagus in the fryer basket.

3. Top the asparagus with salt and pepper and spray it with oil.

4. Toss to coat the seasoning properly.

5. Cook for 9 minutes and serve.

Serving Suggestion: This dish goes well with a slice of lemon and avocado slices.

Variation Tip: You can also add red chili flakes to spice up the dish.

Nutritional Information per Serving:

Calories: 23| **Fat:** 1g| **Sat Fat:** 1g| **Carbohydrates:** 4g|**Fiber:** 2g| **Sugar:** 2g| **Protein:** 3g

Chicken Wings

Preparation Time: 10 minutes
Cooking Time: 45 minutes
Servings: 2

Ingredients:

- 2 pounds chicken wings/drumsticks
- 1 teaspoon salt
- ¼ teaspoon pepper
- 1 tablespoon chili powder
- 1 teaspoon garlic powder
- 1 teaspoon paprika
- 1 teaspoon oregano
- Avocado oil spray

Preparation:

1. Preheat the oven to 425°F.

2. Line a baking sheet with foil and place a baking rack on it.

3. Take a bowl and make the dry seasoning by adding the salt, pepper, chili, paprika, and oregano.

4. Season the wings or drumsticks with the bowl mixture, making sure to coat them thoroughly.

5. Place the coated chicken on the baking rack.

6. Bake for 40 minutes, flipping halfway through.

Serving Suggestion: Serve the chicken with garlic mayo sauce.

Variation Tip: You can add cayenne and white pepper for depth of flavor.

Nutritional Information per Serving:

Calories: 596| **Fat:** 40g| **Sat Fat:** 10g| **Carbohydrates:** 2g|**Fiber:** 2g| **Sugar:** 1g| **Protein:** 46g

Chicken Broccoli Stir Fry

Preparation Time: 15 minutes
Cooking Time: 15 minutes
Servings: 6

Ingredients:

- 2½ pounds boneless chicken, cubed
- 1 teaspoon salt
- ¼ teaspoon pepper
- 4 cups broccoli florets, boiled
- 8 ounce can of water chestnuts
- ¾ cup coconut aminos
- ¼ cup chicken broth
- ½ teaspoon fish sauce
- 1 tablespoon rice wine vinegar
- 1 teaspoon ginger, grated
- 3 cloves garlic, minced
- ¼ teaspoon pepper flakes

Preparation:

1. To make the sauce, take a bowl and add the coconut aminos, fish sauce, chicken broth, rice wine vinegar, ginger, garlic, and pepper flakes, and mix well. Set it aside.

2. Season the chicken with salt and pepper.

3. Take a large skillet and cook the chicken on medium heat.

4. Add in the broccoli and toss for 4 minutes.

5. Add in the sauce and the water chestnuts and cook for 4 minutes.

6. Let the sauce simmer for 2 minutes.

7. Serve and enjoy!

Serving Suggestion: Add a sprinkling of sesame seeds before serving.

Variation Tip: You can add red chili flakes for some spiciness.

Nutritional Information per Serving:

Calories: 294| **Fat:** 5g| **Sat Fat:** 1g| **Carbohydrates:** 10g|**Fiber:** 3g| **Sugar:** 2g| **Protein:** 42g

Cauliflower Mash

Preparation Time: 10 minutes
Cooking Time: 10 minutes
Servings: 4

Ingredients:

- 1 large cauliflower, boiled and cut into florets
- ½ teaspoon salt
- ¼ teaspoon pepper
- 2 tablespoons ghee butter
- ½ cup unsweetened, nut milk creamer

Preparation:

1. Put all the ingredients into a food processor.

2. Start to blend until the desired consistency is reached.

3. Garnish with parsley and serve.

Serving Suggestion: Top the mash with some chopped cilantro and chives.

Variation Tip: Add dried cumin to the ingredients to enhance the taste of the mash.

Nutritional Information per Serving:

Calories: 128| **Fat:** 10g| **Sat Fat:** 6g| **Carbohydrates:** 7g|**Fiber:** 3g| **Sugar:** 3g| **Protein:** 4g

Chicken Salad

Preparation Time: 15 minutes
Cooking Time: 30 minutes
Servings: 4

Ingredients:

- 2 cups chicken, cooked and shredded
- 1 apple, cubed
- 2 tablespoons dried cranberries
- ¼ cup celery, chopped
- ¼ cup pecan halves
- ½ cup mayo
- 1 teaspoon apple cider
- 2 tablespoons tarragon, chopped
- 2 tablespoons onions, chopped
- ½ teaspoon salt
- ¼ teaspoon black pepper

Preparation:

1. Take a bowl and add the apple, chicken, celery, cranberries, and pecans, and toss well.

2. Take another bowl and add the vinegar, mayo, tarragon, salt, pepper, and onions. Mix well.

3. Combine both the mixtures in a large bowl and mix well.

Serving Suggestion: You can place the chicken salad in lettuce wraps.

Variation Tip: If you prefer, use cooked, shredded turkey instead of chicken.

Nutritional Information per Serving:

Calories: 414| **Fat:** 31g| **Sat Fat:** 5g| **Carbohydrates:** 16g|**Fiber:** 3g| **Sugar:** 7g| **Protein:** 19g

Lime Coconut Chicken

Preparation Time: 5 minutes
Cooking Time: 20 minutes
Servings: 4

Ingredients:

- 4 chicken breasts
- 2 tablespoons coconut oil
- ¼ cup chicken stock
- ¼ cup lime juice
- 1½ cup canned coconut milk
- 1 tablespoon garlic, minced
- ½ teaspoon salt
- ½ teaspoon pepper
- ⅛ cup cilantro, chopped

Preparation:

1. Take a large skillet and place it over medium heat.

2. Add the oil and heat it for a while.

3. Season the chicken breasts with salt and pepper and add to the skillet.

4. Cook for 4 to 5 minutes on each side until they are cooked completely.

5. Lower the heat and remove the chicken from the skillet. Set chicken aside.

6. Add the chicken stock, lime juice, coconut milk, garlic, salt, and pepper to the skillet. Stir continuously, scraping up the browned bits from the pan from when the chicken was cooked.

7. Add the chicken back to the skillet with the sauce. Cover and let simmer on medium to medium-low heat for 5 minutes.

8. Remove all the ingredients from the skillet and top with the cilantro.

Serving Suggestion: Serve with your favorite veggies on the side.

Variation Tip: Avocado oil can also be used instead.

Nutritional Information per Serving:

Calories: 407| **Fat:** 31g| **Sat Fat:** 25g| **Carbohydrates:** 7g|**Fiber:** 2g| **Sugar:** 2g| **Protein:** 26g

Chicken Pie Soup

Preparation Time: 10 minutes
Cooking Time: 20 minutes
Servings: 4

Ingredients:

- 2 chicken breasts, cubed
- 2 tablespoons coconut oil
- 1 cup onion, diced
- 1 cup carrots, diced
- 1 cup celery stalks, diced
- 6 cloves garlic, minced
- 12 potatoes, diced
- 2 cups chicken broth
- 1 cup milk
- 1 cup cashews
- 2 tablespoons thyme leaves
- 1½ teaspoons salt
- 1½ teaspoons dried sage
- Black pepper to taste

Preparation:

1. Heat the oil in a large saucepan over medium heat.

2. Sauté the onions, carrots, garlic, and celery until the onions are soft

3. Add in the potatoes, broth, sage, and thyme.

4. Bring the mixture to a boil and then simmer for 4 minutes.

5. Add the chicken and cook for 6 minutes.

6. In a blender, put in the cashews and milk.

7. Blend until a creamy texture is formed.

8. Add the mixture to the saucepan and mix well.

9. Serve hot.

Serving Suggestion: Sprinkle some parsley and chopped red chili on top.

Variation Tip: Use ghee instead of coconut oil.

Nutritional Information per Serving:

Calories: 446 | **Fat:** 24g|**Sat Fat:** 8g|**Carbohydrates:** 40g|**Fiber:** 7g|**Sugar:** 7g|**Protein:** 22g

Thai Chicken Coconut Soup

Preparation Time: 15 minutes
Cooking Time: 40 minutes
Servings: 6

Ingredients:

- 1 tablespoon coconut oil
- ½ onion, sliced
- 2 cloves garlic, chopped
- ½ red jalapeno pepper, sliced
- 11/2 tablespoons ginger, grated
- 1 lemongrass stalk
- 2 teaspoons red Thai curry paste
- 4 cups chicken broth
- 4 cups coconut milk
- 2 medium chicken breasts, cubed
- 8 ounces white mushroom caps, sliced
- 2 tablespoons coconut sugar
- 2 tablespoons fish sauce
- 3 tablespoons lime juice
- 2 scallions, sliced

Preparation:

1. Take a pot and place it over medium heat.

2. Add in the oil, garlic, scallions, ginger, curry paste, and lemongrass.

3. Mix well and cook for 5 minutes.

4. Add in the broth, bring it to a boil, and let it simmer for 30 minutes.

5. Strain out the garlic, lemongrass, ginger, and scallions.

6. Add in the remaining ingredients and simmer until the chicken is cooked.

7. Cook for 2 more minutes and serve.

Serving Suggestion: Sprinkle with chopped cilantro or basil.

Variation Tip: If you prefer, use prawns instead of chicken.

Nutritional Information per Serving:

Calories: 668 | **Fat:** 60g|**Sat Fat:** 51g|**Carbohydrates:** 16g|**Fiber:** 4g|**Sugar:** 1g|**Protein:** 24g

Chicken Soup

Preparation Time: 15 minutes
Cooking Time: 20 minutes
Servings: 4

Ingredients:

- 2 chicken breasts
- 1½ teaspoon salt
- 2 cans tomatoes with green chiles
- 1 can chicken broth (30 Days Whole Foods-compliant)
- 1 medium onion, chopped
- 2 teaspoons garlic powder
- 1 teaspoon onion powder
- 1 teaspoon cumin
- 2 teaspoons chili powder
- 1 teaspoon dried oregano
- 1 teaspoon smoked paprika
- 2 zucchinis, chopped
- 1 can full-fat coconut milk

Preparation:

1. Season the chicken with salt and put it into a pressure cooker.

2. Add in the remaining ingredients.

3. Close the lid.

4. Cook for 18 minutes at high pressure.

5. Let the pressure release for 10 minutes naturally.

6. Select the sauté mode and cook for another 2 to 3 minutes.

7. Serve hot.

Serving Suggestion: Add chopped parsley right before serving.

Variation Tip: Coconut cream can also be used instead of milk for a creamier flavor.

Nutritional Information per Serving:

Calories: 324 | **Fat:** 25g|**Sat Fat:** 20g|**Carbohydrates:** 12g|**Fiber:** 2g|**Sugar:** 3g|**Protein:** 16g

Healthy Toscana Soup

Preparation Time: 10 minutes
Cooking Time: 20 minutes
Servings: 6

Ingredients:

- 4 slices 30 Days Whole Foods-compliant bacon, cooked
- 1 pound Italian sausage
- ½ teaspoon crushed red pepper flakes
- 4 potatoes, diced
- 1 onion, diced
- 2 tablespoons garlic, minced
- 4 cups chicken stock
- ½ bunch kale, stems removed and chopped
- 1 can coconut milk
- Salt to taste
- Pepper to taste

Preparation:

1. Add all ingredients into a pressure cooker.

2. Close the lid.

3. Cook for 20 minutes at high pressure.

4. Let the pressure release for 10 minutes naturally.

5. Select the sauté mode and cook for 2 to 3 minutes.

6. Serve hot and enjoy.

Serving Suggestion: Add a sprinkling of chopped cilantro.

Variation Tip: Coconut cream can be used instead of milk for added creaminess.

Nutritional Information per Serving:

Calories: 394 | **Fat:** 24g|**Sat Fat:** 16g|**Carbohydrates:** 35g|**Fiber:** 5g|**Sugar:** 5g|**Protein:** 13g

Tomato Soup

Preparation Time: 15 minutes
Cooking Time: 10 minutes
Servings: 8

Ingredients:

- 1 tablespoon avocado oil
- ½ cup onion, chopped
- 2 carrots, chopped
- 4 cloves garlic, minced
- 1 tablespoon tomato paste
- 1 can whole San Marzano tomato, crushed
- 2 cups chicken broth
- ½ teaspoon dried thyme
- 1 bay leaf
- 2 tablespoons coconut aminos
- 1 can full-fat coconut cream
- Sea salt to taste
- ¼ cup basil, chopped
- Pepper to taste

Preparation:

1. Add all the ingredients to a pressure cooker.

2. Close the lid.

3. Cook for 15 minutes at high pressure.

4. Let the pressure be quickly released.

5. Serve hot.

Serving Suggestion: Add a swirl of coconut cream and some parsley for garnish.

Variation Tip: Coconut milk can be used instead of cream for a lighter taste and texture.

Nutritional Information per Serving:

Calories: 175 | **Fat:** 13g|**Sat Fat:** 10g|**Carbohydrates:** 13g|**Fiber:** 2g|**Sugar:** 4g|**Protein:** 6g

Broccoli Soup

Preparation Time: 10 minutes
Cooking Time: 20 minutes
Servings: 4

Ingredients:

- 2 tablespoons avocado oil
- 1 small onion, diced
- 2 cloves garlic, minced
- 2 cups chicken stock
- 4 cups broccoli florets
- 1½ cups carrots, shredded
- 1 cup raw cashews
- 1 cup water
- ½ teaspoon mustard powder
- ½ teaspoon smoked paprika
- ½ cup nutritional yeast
- 1 tablespoon lemon juice
- ¼ cup almond milk
- Sea salt to taste
- Pepper to taste

Preparation:

1. Add all the ingredients to a pressure cooker.

2. Close the lid.

3. Cook for 15 minutes at high pressure.

4. Let the pressure quickly release.

5. Serve hot and enjoy.

Serving Suggestion: Garnish with chopped parsley and scallions.

Variation Tip: You can use cauliflower florets instead of broccoli.

Nutritional Information per Serving:

Calories: 333 | **Fat:** 22g|**Sat Fat:** 3g|**Carbohydrates:** 27g|**Fiber:** 6g|**Sugar:** 8g|**Protein:** 12g

Buffalo Chicken Chowder

Preparation Time: 10 minutes
Cooking Time: 4 hours
Servings: 6

Ingredients:

- ½ pound chicken breast
- 1 onion, chopped
- 1 cup celery, diced
- 1 cup carrots, diced
- ½ cup potatoes, diced
- 5 cups chicken broth
- ¾ cup Buffalo Hot Sauce
- ⅔ cup full-fat coconut milk

Preparation:

1. Add all the ingredients to a slow cooker.

2. Close the lid and cook on low for 4 hours.

3. Serve hot.

Serving Suggestion: Sprinkle some cilantro leaves on top.

Variation Tip: Unsweetened nut creamer can be used instead of coconut milk.

Nutritional Information per Serving:

Calories: 253 | **Fat:** 9g|**Sat Fat:** 5g|**Carbohydrates:** 16g|**Fiber:** 2g|**Sugar:** 3g|**Protein:** 27g

Cauliflower Rice Chicken Curry

Preparation Time: 20 minutes
Cooking Time: 20 minutes
Servings: 4

Ingredients:

* 3 cups cauliflower rice
* 3 tablespoons curry powder
* 1 teaspoon garlic powder
* 2 teaspoons turmeric powder
* ½ teaspoon cumin
* ½ teaspoon paprika
* ¼ teaspoon sea salt
* 3 tablespoons coconut oil
* ¾ cup onion, chopped
* 1 teaspoon garlic, minced
* 2 teaspoons coconut oil
* 8 kale leaves, chopped
* 2 cups carrots, chopped
* 4 cups chicken broth
* 1 cup coconut milk
* ½ teaspoon red pepper
* ½ teaspoon black pepper

Preparation:

1. Add all ingredients to a pressure cooker.

2. Close the lid.

3. Cook for 20 minutes at high pressure.

4. Let the pressure quickly release.

5. Serve hot and enjoy.

Serving Suggestion: Sprinkle with cilantro leaves on top.

Variation Tip: Avocado oil can be used instead of coconut oil.

Nutritional Information per Serving:

Calories: 166 | **Fat:** 9g|**Sat Fat:** 1g|**Carbohydrates:** 20g|**Fiber:** 9g|**Sugar:** 7g|**Protein:** 10g

Ginger Carrot Soup

Preparation Time: 20 minutes
Cooking Time: 30 minutes
Servings: 5

Ingredients:

- 1 tablespoon coconut oil
- 1 onion, chopped
- 1 garlic clove, minced
- 3 tablespoons ginger, chopped
- 1 pound carrots, peeled and chopped
- 2 cups vegetable broth
- 1 can coconut milk
- Salt to taste

Preparation:

1. Take a large skillet, place it over medium heat, and heat up the oil.

2. Add in the ginger, onion, and garlic and cook for 5 minutes.

3. Add the remaining ingredients to the skillet and cook for 25 minutes.

4. Using an immersion blender, carefully blend the mixture into a smooth soup.

5. Serve hot and enjoy.

Serving Suggestion: Use fresh mint leaves as a garnish

Variation Tip: Avocado oil can also be used instead.

Nutritional Information per Serving:

Calories: 281 | **Fat:** 23g|**Sat Fat:** 20g|**Carbohydrates:** 17g|**Fiber:** 4g|**Sugar:** 9g|**Protein:** 3g

Stuffed Pepper Soup

Preparation Time: 10 minutes
Cooking Time: 10 minutes
Servings: 6

Ingredients:

- 2 tablespoons avocado oil
- 1 onion, diced
- 3 cloves garlic, minced
- ½ pound ground beef, cooked
- 2 teaspoons Italian seasoning
- Salt to taste
- 2 green bell peppers, diced
- 1 red bell pepper, diced
- 1 can fire-roasted diced tomatoes
- 1 can tomato sauce
- 3 cups beef broth
- ¼ cup red wine vinegar

Preparation:

1. Add all the ingredients to a pressure cooker.
2. Close the lid.
3. Cook for 10 minutes at high pressure.
4. Let the pressure quickly release.
5. Serve hot.

Serving Suggestion: Cauliflower rice is the perfect side dish.

Variation Tip: Coconut oil can be used instead.

Nutritional Information per Serving:

Calories: 378 | **Fat:** 28g|**Sat Fat:** 9g|**Carbohydrates:** 8g|**Fiber:** 3g|**Sugar:** 4g|**Protein:** 23g

Lemon Pepper Salmon

Preparation Time: 10 minutes
Cooking Time: 10 minutes
Servings: 4

Ingredients:

- ¾ cup water
- A few sprigs of parsley
- ½ pound salmon filet
- 2 tablespoons ghee
- ¼ teaspoon salt
- ½ teaspoon pepper
- ½ lemon, thinly sliced

Preparation:

1. Add all the ingredients to a pressure cooker.

2. Close the lid.

3. Select the steam function and steam for 3 minutes.

4. Let the pressure quickly release.

5. Serve hot.

Serving Suggestion: Add chopped dill, chopped pickles, and a squeeze of lemon.

Variation Tip: Substitute the salmon for another fish of your choice.

Nutritional Information per Serving:

Calories: 340 | **Fat:** 20g|**Sat Fat:** 8g|**Carbohydrates:** 8g|**Fiber:** 3g|**Sugar:** 5g|**Protein:** 32g

Broccoli Salad

Preparation Time: 10 minutes
Cooking Time: 0 minutes
Servings: 4

Ingredients:

- 2 cups broccoli florets, boiled
- ½ cup scallions, chopped
- ⅓ cup roasted cashews
- 2 tablespoons sesame seeds
- ¼ cup almond butter
- 1 clove garlic, minced
- 2 tablespoons lime juice
- 2 tablespoons sesame oil
- 3 tablespoons coconut aminos

Preparation:

1. Take a large bowl and add all ingredients to it.

2. Toss well until well combined.

3. Serve immediately.

Serving Suggestion: Drizzle some olive oil on top.

Variation Tip: You can add other chopped nuts and seeds.

Nutritional Information per Serving:

Calories: 360 | **Fat:** 22g|**Sat Fat:** 0g|**Carbohydrates:** 23g|**Fiber:** 0g|**Sugar:** 10g|**Protein:** 15g

Roast Beef

Preparation Time: 20 minutes
Cooking Time: 2 hours
Servings: 6

Ingredients:

- 4 pounds round roast
- ¼ cup avocado oil
- 3 cloves garlic, minced
- 1 tablespoon rosemary
- 1 tablespoon thyme leaves, chopped
- 2 teaspoons kosher salt
- Pepper to taste

Preparation:

1. Preheat the oven to 450°F.

2. Take a bowl and add the oil, garlic, thyme, pepper, salt, and rosemary and mix well.

3. Rub the roast with all the mixture.

4. Place the roast on a roasting rack and into the oven.

5. Reduce the heat to 325°F.

6. Roast for 2 hours.

Serving Suggestion: Serve the roast with roasted sweet potatoes.

Variation Tip: Add red chili to the roast rub if you prefer some heat.

Nutritional Information per Serving:

Calories: 231| **Fat:** 10g|**Sat Fat:** 4g|**Carbohydrates:** 34g|**Fiber:** 4g|**Sugar:** 4g|**Protein:** 23g

Butternut Squash Hash

Preparation Time: 15 minutes
Cooking Time: 25 minutes
Servings: 4

Ingredients:

- 1½ tablespoons coconut oil
- 1 medium onion, diced
- 1 small butternut squash, diced
- 1 apple, diced
- 12 ounces ground turkey, cooked
- ½ teaspoon dried sage
- ¼ teaspoon dried thyme
- ¼ teaspoon garlic powder
- Salt to taste
- Pinch of nutmeg
- 3 cups kale, torn

Preparation:

1. Take a large skillet and place it over medium heat.

2. Add in the oil and butternut squash and sauté for 8 minutes.

3. Add in the apple and cook for 5 more minutes, stirring occasionally.

4. Add in the remaining ingredients and cook for a further 6 minutes.

5. Right at the end, add the kale and cook for 2 more minutes.

6. Mix well and serve.

Serving Suggestion: Serve with a fried egg on top.

Variation Tip: Add crushed red chili flakes for a kick of spice and heat.

Nutritional Information per Serving:

Calories: 308 | **Fat:** 13g|**Sat Fat:** 0g|**Carbohydrates:** 24g|**Fiber:** 5g|**Sugar:** 8g|**Protein:** 25g

Brussels Sprouts Chicken Skillet

Preparation Time: 20 minutes
Cooking Time: 15 minutes
Servings: 4

Ingredients:

* 1 tablespoon olive oil
* 1 pound chicken breasts, cubed
* 1 teaspoon kosher salt
* ½ teaspoon black pepper
* 3 cups Brussels sprouts, trimmed
* 1 sweet potato, peeled, cubed, and boiled
* 1 onion, chopped
* 2 apples, cubed
* 4 cloves garlic, minced
* 2 teaspoons thyme, chopped
* 1 teaspoon ground cinnamon
* 1 cup reduced-sodium chicken broth

Preparation:

1. Heat the oil in a large skillet over medium heat.

2. Add the chicken, salt, and pepper and cook until the chicken is cooked through.

3. Add in the remaining ingredients and cook for 10 minutes, stirring occasionally.

4. Bring the broth to a simmer and let it evaporate.

5. Serve and enjoy.

Serving Suggestion: Drizzle hot sauce on top.

Variation Tip: Pork also works great with this dish.

Nutritional Information per Serving:

Calories: 435 | **Fat:** 21g|**Sat Fat:** 6g|**Carbohydrates:** 30g|**Fiber:** 7g|**Sugar:** 14g|**Protein:** 32g

Lemon Chicken

Preparation Time: 8 minutes
Cooking Time: 17 minutes
Servings: 3

Ingredients:

- 1 tablespoon olive oil
- 1 tablespoon fresh parsley, minced
- ½ pound skinless and boneless chicken breasts
- ½ teaspoon fresh lemon zest, grated finely
- 1 garlic clove, minced
- ½ pound yellow squash, sliced
- 1 tablespoon fresh lemon juice
- Salt and pepper, to taste

Preparation:

1. Take a skillet and place it over medium heat.

2. Add the oil to it and let it warm.

3. Add in the chicken and cook for 8 minutes until it is cooked through.

4. Take out the chicken and set it aside.

5. In the same skillet, sauté the garlic for about 1 minute and then add in the squash slices.

6. Cook for about 6 minutes and then add the chicken back to it.

7. Stir well and cook for about 2 minutes.

8. Add the lemon zest, lemon juice, and parsley, and stir well.

Serving Suggestion: Garnish with chopped basil before serving.

Variation Tip: Coconut oil can be used instead.

Nutritional Information per Serving:

Calories: 170 | **Fat:** 7.2g|**Sat Fat:** 1g|**Carbohydrates:** 3.1g|**Fiber:** 0.9g|**Sugar:** 1.5g|**Protein:** 23g

Pepper Chicken

Preparation Time: 15 minutes
Cooking Time: 45 minutes
Servings: 10

Ingredients:

- ¾ pound skinless, boneless chicken thighs
- 2 teaspoons dried rosemary
- 6 broccoli heads, cut into florets
- 2 teaspoons dried oregano, crushed
- 8 garlic cloves, minced
- ½ cup extra-virgin olive oil
- Salt to taste
- 2 teaspoons pepper
- ½ teaspoon white pepper.

Preparation:

1. Preheat the oven to 375°F.

2. Place the chicken thighs, dried rosemary, dried oregano, garlic, salt, pepper, and oil in a large bowl. Toss to coat the chicken well.

3. Arrange the broccoli florets in the bottom of a baking dish and top them with chicken thighs and the seasoning.

4. Bake for 45 minutes.

Serving Suggestion: Sprinkle the cooked chicken with mint leaves.

Variation Tip: You can use turkey instead of chicken.

Nutritional Information per Serving:

Calories: 127 | **Fat:** 9.6g|**Sat Fat:** 2g|**Carbohydrates:** 4g|**Fiber:** 1.4g|**Sugar:** 0.8g|**Protein:** 7g

Veggies with Sausages

Preparation Time: 15 minutes
Cooking Time: 20 minutes
Servings: 4

Ingredients:

- 4 fully cooked chicken sausages
- 16 ounces fresh green beans, trimmed
- 1 cup Brussels sprouts
- 3 tablespoons olive oil
- 1 teaspoon salt
- ½ teaspoon black pepper
- ½ teaspoon garlic powder

Preparation:

1. Preheat the oven to 425°F.

2. Take a bowl and add all the ingredients to it.

3. Toss well until the veggies are fully coated with the mixture.

4. Spread the veggies-sausages mix in a single layer in a large baking dish.

5. Bake for 20 minutes, tossing the mixture halfway through.

Serving Suggestion: Sprinkle with chopped parsley.

Variation Tip: You can add chili sauce for a fiery kick of flavor.

Nutritional Information per Serving:

Calories: 349| **Fat:** 23g|**Sat Fat:** 4g|**Carbohydrates:** 22g|**Fiber:** 7g|**Sugar:** 6g|**Protein:** 20g

Chicken with Avocado Salad

Preparation Time: 15 minutes
Cooking Time: 0 minutes
Servings: 4

Ingredients:

- 2 cups cooked chicken, shredded
- 2 teaspoons Dijon mustard
- 2 avocados, peeled and chopped
- ½ cup coconut cream
- 1 teaspoon lemon juice
- 2 tablespoons fresh lime juice
- ¼ teaspoon cayenne pepper
- Salt, to taste

Preparation:

1. Add the avocados and lime juice to a large bowl. Mash and combine well.

2. Add the coconut cream, cayenne pepper, salt, and Dijon mustard.

3. Add in the shredded chicken and mix well.

4. Serve immediately.

Serving Suggestion: Top with chopped parsley leaves.

Variation Tip: You can add some of your favorite spices to the mixture.

Nutritional Information per Serving:

Calories: 336 | **Fat:** 24g|**Sat Fat:** 4g|**Carbohydrates:** 12g|**Fiber:** 6.9g|**Sugar:** 2g|**Protein:** 25g

Salmon Veg Salad

Preparation Time: 15 minutes
Cooking Time: 0 minutes
Servings: 4

Ingredients:

- 4 salmon filets, cooked
- 4 tablespoons fresh lemon juice
- 2 cups cucumber, sliced
- 4 tablespoons olive oil
- 2 cups red bell pepper, sliced
- 2 cups fresh spinach, torn
- 1 cup grape tomatoes, quartered
- 2 cups lettuce, torn
- 2 tablespoons scallions, chopped
- Salt and black pepper, to taste

Preparation:

1. Take a bowl and add all the ingredients to it except for the salmon.

2. Toss well until all the ingredients are combined well.

3. Add the salmon on top and serve.

Serving Suggestion: Add some slices of lime on the side.

Variation Tip: Instead of salmon, use any other fish you prefer.

Nutritional Information per Serving:

Calories: 491 | **Fat:** 29g|**Sat Fat:** 4g|**Carbohydrates:** 10g|**Fiber:** 2g|**Sugar:** 6g|**Protein:** 50g

Roasted Radish

Preparation Time: 15 minutes
Cooking Time: 15 minutes
Servings: 4

Ingredients:

- 1 pound radishes, halved and without stems
- 1 tablespoon coconut oil
- ½ teaspoon sea salt
- ⅛ teaspoon black pepper
- ¼ teaspoon parsley
- 2 garlic cloves, minced

Preparation:

1. Preheat the oven to 425°F.

2. Take a bowl and add all the ingredients to it.

3. Toss well until the radishes are properly coated.

4. Take a baking dish and add in the radish mixture, spreading it in a single layer.

5. Bake for 20 minutes, tossing the mixture halfway through.

6. Serve and enjoy!

Serving Suggestion: Add a touch of homemade ranch dressing on top.

Variation Tip: Include some dried dill to add an interesting flavor.

Nutritional Information per Serving:

Calories: 68| **Fat:** 6g|**Sat Fat:** 3g|**Carbohydrates:** 4g|**Fiber:** 1g|**Sugar:** 2g|**Protein:** 1g

Roast Potatoes

Preparation Time: 10 minutes
Cooking Time: 20 minutes
Servings: 4

Ingredients:

- 4 potatoes, thickly sliced
- 1 tablespoon coconut oil
- ½ teaspoon sea salt
- ⅛ teaspoon black pepper
- ¼ teaspoon parsley
- 2 garlic cloves, minced

Preparation:

1. Preheat the oven to 425°F.

2. Take a bowl and add all the ingredients to it.

3. Toss well until the potatoes are thoroughly coated.

4. In a large baking dish, spread the potatoes in a single layer.

5. Bake for 20 minutes, tossing the mixture halfway through.

Serving Suggestion: Serve the potatoes with some garlic mayo.

Variation Tip: Add chili flakes to the mixture for spice.

Nutritional Information per Serving:

Calories: 164| **Fat:** 6g|**Sat Fat:** 4g|**Carbohydrates:** 25g|**Fiber:** 3g|**Sugar:** 2g|**Protein:** 4g

Roasted Cauliflower

Preparation Time: 10 minutes
Cooking Time: 20 minutes
Servings: 6

Ingredients:

- 2 ounces cauliflower florets
- ⅓ cup Frank's Red Hot Sauce
- 2 tablespoons coconut oil
- 1 tablespoon coconut aminos
- 1 teaspoon apple cider vinegar
- ½ teaspoon garlic powder
- ¼ teaspoon cayenne pepper

Preparation:

1. Preheat the oven to 425°F.

2. Take a bowl and add all the ingredients to it.

3. Toss well until the cauliflower florets are completely coated.

4. In a baking dish, spread the cauliflower florets in a single layer.

5. Bake for 20 minutes, tossing the mixture halfway through.

6. Serve and enjoy!

Serving Suggestion: Garnish with chopped chives and parsley.

Variation Tip: Avocado oil can be used instead.

Nutritional Information per Serving:

Calories: 95| **Fat:** 5g|**Sat Fat:** 2g|**Carbohydrates:** 11g|**Fiber:** 2g|**Sugar:** 2g|**Protein:** 2g

Thyme Roasted Carrots

Preparation Time: 10 minutes
Cooking Time: 25 minutes
Servings: 6

Ingredients:

- 1 pound carrots, cut into long slices
- 2 tablespoons olive oil
- 2 tablespoons lemon juice
- 2 teaspoons thyme, chopped
- Salt to taste
- Pepper to taste

Preparation:

1. Preheat the oven to 400°F.

2. Add all the ingredients to a bowl.

3. Toss well until the carrots are thoroughly coated.

4. Spread the carrots in a single layer in a large baking dish.

5. Bake for 20 minutes, tossing halfway through.

6. Take out from the oven and serve hot.

Serving Suggestion: Serve with garlic mayo on the side.

Variation Tip: Add vinegar for a sweet-sour taste.

Nutritional Information per Serving:

Calories: 73| **Fat:** 4g|**Sat Fat:** 1g|**Carbohydrates:** 7g|**Fiber:** 2g|**Sugar:** 3g|**Protein:** 2g

Brussels Sprouts

Preparation Time: 15 minutes
Cooking Time: 20 minutes
Servings: 4

Ingredients:

- 16 ounces Brussels sprouts
- 3 tablespoons avocado oil
- Salt to taste
- ¼ teaspoon black pepper

Preparation:

1. Preheat the oven to 425°F.

2. Take a bowl and add all the ingredients to it.

3. Toss well until the Brussels sprouts are thoroughly coated.

4. Spread the sprouts in a single layer in a large baking dish.

5. Bake for 20 minutes, tossing halfway through.

6. Take out from the oven and serve.

Serving Suggestion: Add some garlic mayo on the side.

Variation Tip: White pepper and some chili flakes will add a depth of flavor.

Nutritional Information per Serving:

Calories: 110| **Fat:** 7g|**Sat Fat:** 0.9g|**Carbohydrates:** 11g|**Fiber:** 4g|**Sugar:** 2g|**Protein:** 3g

Green Beans with Roasted Almonds

Preparation Time: 10 minutes
Cooking Time: 20 minutes
Servings: 4

Ingredients:

- 1 pound fresh green beans, trimmed
- 2 tablespoons coconut oil
- Salt to taste
- Pepper to taste
- ¼ cup almonds, roasted and sliced
- 2 teaspoons garlic, minced

Preparation:

1. Preheat the oven to 425°F.

2. Take a bowl and add all the ingredients to it.

3. Toss well until the beans and almonds are seasoned properly.

4. In a baking dish, spread the mixture in a single layer.

5. Bake for 20 minutes, tossing halfway through.

Serving Suggestion: You can drizzle hot sauce on top before serving.

Variation Tip: Add cayenne pepper to enhance the flavor of the beans.

Nutritional Information per Serving:

Calories: 137| **Fat:** 10g|**Sat Fat:** 1g|**Carbohydrates:** 10g|**Fiber:** 3g|**Sugar:** 3g|**Protein:** 3g

Green Beans with Garlic

Preparation Time: 10 minutes
Cooking Time: 13 minutes

Servings: 6

Ingredients:

- 16 ounces green beans, trimmed
- 2 tablespoons olive avocado oil
- 1 tablespoon garlic, minced
- Salt to taste

Preparation:

1. Take a nonstick pan and add the oil. Place it over medium heat.

2. Add in the beans, cover with a lid, and cook for 10 minutes, stirring occasionally.

3. Lower the heat and add in the garlic.

4. Cook for another 2 minutes, top with salt and serve.

Serving Suggestion: You can add some garlic mayo on the side.

Variation Tip: Add cayenne pepper for a hint of spice.

Nutritional Information per Serving:

Calories: 66| **Fat:** 4g|**Sat Fat:** 1g|**Carbohydrates:** 5g|**Fiber:** 2g|**Sugar:** 2g|**Protein:** 1g

Roasted Red Cabbage

Preparation Time: 10 minutes
Cooking Time: 20 minutes
Servings: 8

Ingredients:

- 1 red cabbage, cut into ½-inch slices
- 2 tablespoons avocado oil
- Salt to taste
- Pepper to taste

Preparation:

1. Preheat the oven to 400°F.

2. Add all the ingredients to a bowl.

3. Toss well until the cabbage is fully coated.

4. Spread the cabbage mixture into a baking dish in a single layer.

5. Bake for 20 minutes, tossing halfway through.

6. Take out from the oven and serve.

Serving Suggestion: Drizzle with hot sauce before serving.

Variation Tip: Add dried rosemary to the seasoning for flavor.

Nutritional Information per Serving:

Calories: 79| **Fat:** 4g|**Sat Fat:** 1g|**Carbohydrates:** 9g|**Fiber:** 2g|**Sugar:** 4g|**Protein:** 2g

Mash Potatoes

Preparation Time: 10 minutes
Cooking Time: 15 minutes
Servings: 1

Ingredients:

- 8 potatoes, peeled, boiled, and cubed
- 1½ cups chicken stock
- 2 tablespoons ghee, melted
- Salt to taste
- Pepper to taste

Preparation:

1. Take a blender and add the potatoes along with 1 cup of chicken stock.

2. Blend and then add the remaining stock.

3. Beat until the desired consistency of mash is reached.

4. Add in the butter, salt, and pepper and mix well.

5. Place all of the mash in a bowl.

6. Garnish it and serve.

Serving Suggestion: Top with fresh parsley or mint.

Variation Tip: Add white pepper for a flavor boost.

Nutritional Information per Serving:

Calories: 125| **Fat:** 3g|**Sat Fat:** 1g|**Carbohydrates:** 21g|**Fiber:** 3g|**Sugar:** 1g|**Protein:** 4g

Cilantro Cauliflower Rice

Preparation Time: 15 minutes
Cooking Time: 10 minutes
Servings: 4

Ingredients:

- 1 head of cauliflower, cut into florets
- 1 tablespoon coconut oil
- ½ teaspoon salt
- ½ teaspoon garlic powder
- ¼ cup lime juice
- ⅛ cup cilantro, chopped

Preparation:

1. Add the cauliflower florets to a blender and blend until the texture becomes like rice.

2. Take a skillet, place it over medium heat, and add the oil.

3. Add in the cauliflower rice from the blender and sauté for 1 minute.

4. Keep stirring and gradually add in the remaining ingredients.

5. Close the skillet lid and cook for 5 minutes. Stir occasionally.

6. Serve and enjoy!

Serving Suggestion: You can top the rice with lime wedges.

Variation Tip: Add in chili flakes to enhance the flavor.

Nutritional Information per Serving:

Calories: 40| **Fat:** 3g|**Sat Fat:** 1g|**Carbohydrates:** 3g|**Fiber:** 2g|**Sugar:** 0.4g|**Protein:** 0.6g

Strawberry Ice Cream

Preparation Time: 10 minutes
Cooking Time: 0 minutes
Servings: 2 scoops

Ingredients:

- ½ cup coconut cream
- ½ cup coconut or almond milk
- ½ cup orange juice
- 3 dates, pitted
- 1 tablespoon vanilla extract
- 2 cups frozen strawberries
- 1 cup of ice cubes

Preparation:

1. Add all the ingredients to a blender. Blend well.

2. Take out the mixture, place it in a Tupperware box, and let it freeze for 3 hours or more.

Serving Suggestion: Serve with chopped nuts and mint leaves on top.

Variation Tip: This ice cream recipe works well with any kind of berries.

Nutritional Information per Serving:

Calories: 645| **Fat:** 42.2g|**Sat Fat:** 37.2g|**Carbohydrates:** 63.5g|**Fiber:** 14.4g|**Sugar:** 45.4g|**Protein:** 5g

Chia Coconut Pudding

Preparation Time: 15 minutes
Cooking Time: 0 minutes
Servings: 2

Ingredients:

- ¼ cup unsweetened coconut, shredded
- ¼ cup chia seeds
- ¾ cup coconut milk
- ½ cup coconut water
- 1 teaspoon vanilla extract
- ¼ teaspoon salt
- ½ cup raspberries, fresh

Preparation:

1. Take a bowl and place all the ingredients except for the raspberries in it.

2. Mix well until combined.

3. Place in serving glasses and put in the refrigerator for 2 to 3 hours.

4. Serve with the raspberries on top.

Serving Suggestion: You can sprinkle some shredded coconut over the dessert.

Variation Tip: You can use strawberries or blueberries instead of raspberries.

Nutritional Information per Serving:

Calories: 265| **Fat:** 25g|**Sat Fat:** 22g|**Carbohydrates:** 10.5g|**Fiber:** 4.9g|**Sugar:** 5.3g|**Protein:** 2.8g

Mango Banana Ice Cream

Preparation Time: 15 minutes0
Cooking Time: 0 minutes
Servings: 2

Ingredients:

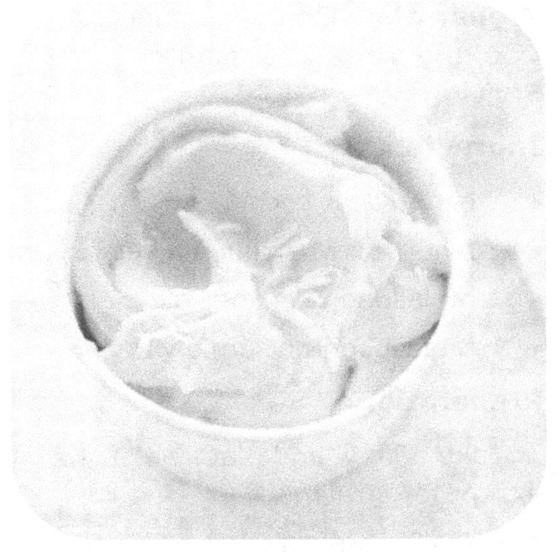

- 1 frozen banana
- 2 cups frozen mangos
- ⅓ cup coconut milk

Preparation:

1. Let the frozen fruits thaw for 10 minutes.

2. Take a blender and add in all the ingredients.

3. Blend until the mixture is smooth and creamy.

4. Freeze for 3 to 4 hours or overnight.

5. Serve and enjoy!

Serving Suggestion: Add shredded coconut on top.

Variation Tip: You can use peaches instead of mango if you prefer.

Nutritional Information per Serving:

Calories: 114| **Fat:** 4g|**Sat Fat:** 4g|**Carbohydrates:** 20g|**Fiber:** 2g|**Sugar:** 15g|**Protein:** 2g

Strawberry Coconut Cream

Preparation Time: 15 minutes
Cooking Time: 20 minutes
Servings: 4

Ingredients:

- 1 can full-fat coconut milk
- 2 pints strawberries, halved and roasted
- 1 tablespoon coconut oil
- 1 tablespoon balsamic vinegar

Preparation:

1. Take a bowl and place all of the ingredients in it except for strawberries.

2. Mix well until the texture is creamy.

3. Place the mixture in serving bowls and add the roasted strawberries on top.

Serving Suggestion: You can add a little coconut cream on top.

Variation Tip: Use pineapple instead of strawberries.

Nutritional Information per Serving:

Calories: 147| **Fat:** 9.9g|**Sat Fat:** 8.4g|**Carbohydrates:** 15g|**Fiber:** 3.6g|**Sugar:** 9.3g|**Protein:** 1.7g

Sweet Fruit Salad

Preparation Time: 20 minutes
Cooking Time: 0 minutes
Servings: 10

Ingredients:

- ¼ cup pineapple juice
- ¼ cup orange juice
- 1 cup strawberries, halved and hulled
- 1 cup blueberries
- 1 cup raspberries
- 3 kiwis, peeled and sliced
- 2 apples, peeled and cubed
- 2 cups grapes
- 1 mango, peeled and cubed

Preparation:

1. Take a large bowl and place all the ingredients in it.

2. Toss well until everything is combined.

3. Place into the refrigerator for 1 to 2 hours.

4. Serve and enjoy.

Serving Suggestion: Serve with fresh lime juice and some mint leaves.

Variation Tip: Use other fruit juices if you prefer.

Nutritional Information per Serving:

Calories: 117| **Fat:** 0.6g|**Sat Fat:** 0.1g|**Carbohydrates:** 30g|**Fiber:** 3.9g|**Sugar:** 24.4g|**Protein:** 1.2g

Avocado Ice Cream

Preparation Time: 15 minutes
Cooking Time: 0 minutes
Servings: 10

Ingredients:

- 4 avocados, pitted and peeled
- 1 cup lime juice
- 1 cup Medjool dates
- 1 cup water
- 2 cans coconut cream
- 2 teaspoons vanilla essence
- 2 teaspoons coconut oil
- ½ teaspoon kosher salt

Preparation:

1. Let the frozen fruits thaw for 10 minutes.

2. Take a blender and add all ingredients to it.

3. Blend until the texture is creamy and smooth.

4. Freeze for 3 to 4 hours or overnight.

Serving Suggestion: Fresh mint leaves go perfectly with this dish.

Variation Tip: You can use coconut water for variation.

Nutritional Information per Serving:

Calories: 469| **Fat:** 26.3g|**Sat Fat:** 13.3g|**Carbohydrates:** 60g|**Fiber:** 5.5g|**Sugar:** 49.8g|**Protein:** 2.2g

Coconut Chocolate Pudding

Preparation Time: 10 minutes
Cooking Time: 10 minutes
Servings: 2

Ingredients:

- 1½ cups coconut cream
- ¼ cup cacao powder
- 3 tablespoons date syrup
- 1 teaspoon vanilla extract
- ¼ teaspoon sea salt

Preparation:

1. Take a small saucepan and place on medium heat.

2. Add ¾ cup of the coconut cream and all of the date syrup and cacao powder.

3. Cook for 5 minutes, stirring often.

4. After the mixture is slightly thickened, add in the vanilla extract and sea salt. Stir well.

5. Pour the syrup into a jar and place it into serving bowls.

6. Whisk the remaining ¾ cup of coconut cream and place it over the pudding.

Serving Suggestion: Add some shredded coconut on top.

Variation Tip: Use a ¼ teaspoon of cinnamon or ginger to add another layer of flavor to the dish.

Nutritional Information per Serving:

Calories: 152| **Fat:** 157.4g|**Sat Fat:** 139g|**Carbohydrates:** 38g|**Fiber:** 14g|**Sugar:** 23.3g|**Protein:** 15g

Caramel Apples

Preparation Time: 10 minutes
Cooking Time: 5 minutes
Servings: 2

Ingredients:

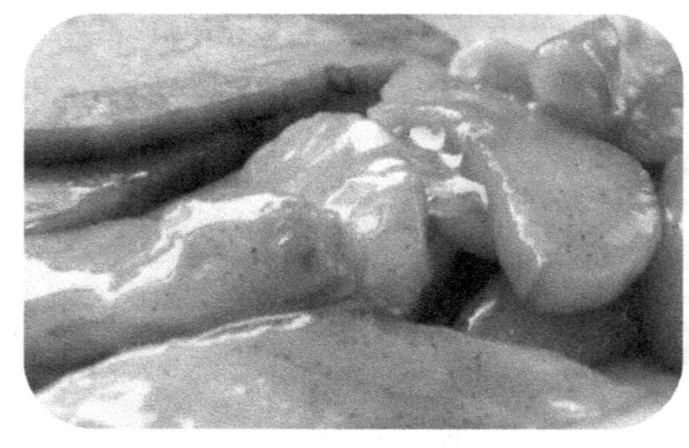

- 1 tablespoon coconut oil
- 2 medium apples, peeled and sliced
- 1 teaspoon ground cinnamon
- ½ cup coconut cream
- ¼ cup date syrup
- ¼ teaspoon kosher salt

Preparation:

1. Take a skillet and place it over medium heat.

2. Add in the apples, cook for 5 minutes until they become soft, and then set aside.

3. Take a blender and add all the remaining ingredients to it.

4. Blend the ingredients until they are completely whipped.

5. Place the apples on a serving plate and drizzle the sauce over them.

Serving Suggestion: Sprinkle some cinnamon on top.

Variation Tip: You can add chopped nuts to the dessert.

Nutritional Information per Serving:

Calories: 316| **Fat:** 21.5g|**Sat Fat:** 18.6g|**Carbohydrates:** 35.1g|**Fiber:** 7.3g|**Sugar:** 25g|**Protein:** 2g

Blueberry Delight

Preparation Time: 10 minutes
Cooking Time: 25 minutes
Servings: 4

Ingredients:

- 2 pints fresh blueberries
- 1 lemon juice
- 4 tablespoons tapioca flour
- ¾ cup almond flour
- 1 teaspoon baking powder
- ¼ teaspoon salt
- ¼ cup date syrup
- ¼ cup coconut oil
- 2 tablespoons coconut milk

Preparation:

1. Preheat the oven to 375°F.

2. Take a bowl and add the lemon juice, blueberries, and 2 tablespoons of the tapioca flour. Mix well.

3. Divide this mixture into small ceramic ramekins.

4. Take another bowl and add the remaining tapioca flour, baking powder, salt, almond flour, coconut oil, coconut milk, and date syrup. Mix and combine well.

5. Divide this mixture equally onto the berry mixture in the ramekins.

6. Bake for 25 minutes.

7. Take out and let cool for a few minutes.

Serving Suggestion: Serve with homemade date sauce.

Variation Tip: Almond milk can be used instead of coconut milk.

Nutritional Information per Serving:

Calories: 283| **Fat:** 16.2g|**Sat Fat:** 13.4g|**Carbohydrates:** 38g|**Fiber:** 5.1g|**Sugar:** 24.4g|**Protein:** 1.8g

Avocado Mousse

Preparation Time: 10 minutes
Cooking Time: 0 minutes
Servings: 2

Ingredients:

- ½ cup coconut milk
- 1 cup cashews, soaked overnight
- ½ cup date syrup
- 2 avocados, peeled
- 4 limes, juiced
- Pinch of sea salt

Preparation:

1. Take a blender and add all ingredients to it.

2. Blend until a creamy texture is formed.

3. Place into serving bowls or glasses and refrigerate for 1 to 2 hours.

Serving Suggestion: Serve with shredded coconut on top.

Variation Tip: Almond milk can be used instead.

Nutritional Information per Serving:

Calories: 899| **Fat:** 71.1g|**Sat Fat:** 14.6g|**Carbohydrates:** 65g|**Fiber:** 16g|**Sugar:** 22.4g|**Protein:** 15g

Basic Dressings, Sauces, and Condiments Recipes

Balsamic Salad Dressing

Preparation Time: 5 minutes
Cooking Time: 0 minutes
Servings: 2 cups

Ingredients:

- ¼ cup balsamic vinegar
- 2 cloves garlic, crushed
- ½ cup avocado oil
- 1 tablespoon Dijon mustard
- ½ teaspoon sea salt
- ½ teaspoon crushed black pepper

Preparation:

1. Add all the ingredients to a bowl and mix well.

2. Store in the refrigerator in an airtight container and use when required. Consume before 2 weeks.

Serving Suggestion: Drizzle it on any salad and enjoy.

Variation Tip: Coconut oil can also be used instead of avocado oil.

Nutritional Information per Serving:

Calories: 92| **Fat:** 7.5g|**Sat Fat:** 1.5g|**Carbohydrates:** 5.2g|**Fiber:** 2.9g|**Sugar:** 0.4g|**Protein:** 1.3g

Sesame Dressing

Preparation Time: 10 minutes
Cooking Time: 5 minutes
Servings: 4

Ingredients:

- ¼ cup coconut aminos
- 2 tablespoons avocado oil
- 2 tablespoons rice vinegar
- ½ tablespoon sesame oil
- 1 teaspoon garlic, minced
- 1 teaspoon ginger, grated
- 2 dates, soaked

Preparation:

1. Take a blender and add every ingredient to it.

2. Process until a creamy texture is formed.

3. Store in an airtight container and consume within 3 to 4 days.

Serving Suggestion: Serve with any salad of your choice.

Variation Tip: You can add cayenne pepper for a flavor kick.

Nutritional Information per Serving:

Calories: 145| **Fat:** 8g|**Sat Fat:** 1g|**Carbohydrates:** 18g|**Fiber:** 1g|**Sugar:** 10g|**Protein:** 1g

Burger Sauce

Preparation Time: 10 minutes
Cooking Time: 10 minutes
Servings: 4

Ingredients:

- ⅓ cup mayo
- 2 tablespoons dill pickles
- 2 tablespoons no-sugar ketchup
- ½ tablespoon onion, minced
- ½ tablespoon coconut aminos
- 1 teaspoon dill pickle juice
- ½ teaspoon garlic powder
- ½ teaspoon paprika
- ½ teaspoon salt
- ¼ teaspoon black pepper

Preparation:

1. Add every ingredient to a bowl and mix well.

2. Store in an airtight container in the refrigerator and consume within 1 month.

Serving Suggestion: Serve with lean beef mince burgers.

Variation Tip: You can add red chili powder for a spicy kick of flavor.

Nutritional Information per Serving:

Calories: 142| **Fat:** 16g|**Sat Fat:** 2g|**Carbohydrates:** 2.1g|**Fiber:** 0g|**Sugar:** 0g|**Protein:** 0.2g

Lemon Dressing

Preparation Time: 10 minutes
Cooking Time: 0 minutes
Servings: 1 cup

Ingredients:

- 2 lemons, juiced
- 1 tablespoon white vinegar
- ½ tablespoon Dijon mustard
- 1 garlic clove, minced
- ½ cup avocado oil

Preparation:

1. Add every ingredient to a bowl and mix well.

2. Store in an airtight container in the refrigerator and use it when you want. Consume within 2 weeks.

Serving Suggestion: Serve it with grilled asparagus.

Variation Tip: Coconut oil can also be used instead of avocado oil.

Nutritional Information per Serving:

Calories: 62| **Fat:** 6.8g|**Sat Fat:** 0.9g|**Carbohydrates:** 0.8g|**Fiber:** 0.2g|**Sugar:** 0.2g|**Protein:** 0.1g

Ranch Dressing

Preparation Time: 10 minutes
Cooking Time: 0 minutes
Servings: 2 cups

Ingredients:

- 1 cup paleo mayonnaise
- ½ cup parsley, chopped
- 4 tablespoons lemon juice
- 4 cloves garlic, minced
- 2 tablespoons dill, chopped
- 1 teaspoon lemon zest
- ½ teaspoon sea salt
- Pepper to taste

Preparation:

1. Take a blender and add all the ingredients to it.

2. Blend until smooth.

3. Store in the refrigerator in an airtight container and use when required. Consume within a week.

Serving Suggestion: This sauce goes well with raw, chopped veggies.

Variation Tip: Himalayan salt can also be used.

Nutritional Information per Serving:

Calories: 81| **Fat:** 9g|**Sat Fat:** 1g|**Carbohydrates:** 1g|**Fiber:** 0.2g|**Sugar:** 0.1g|**Protein:** 0.4g

Cashew Curry Dip

Preparation Time: 10 minutes
Cooking Time: 0 minutes
Servings: 1 cup

Ingredients:

- ½ cup cashews, soaked and drained
- 1½ tablespoons red curry paste
- 1 tablespoon coconut aminos
- 2 tablespoons lime juice
- ½ teaspoon garlic powder
- ½ teaspoon red pepper flakes
- ½ teaspoon ground ginger
- ¼ cup water
- Salt to taste

Preparation:

1. Take a blender and add all the ingredients to it.

2. Blend until smooth.

3. Store in an airtight container in the refrigerator and use when required. The sauce should keep for around 2 weeks.

Serving Suggestion: Serve as a side with chicken skewers.

Variation Tip: Add black pepper for taste variation.

Nutritional Information per Serving:

Calories: 50| **Fat:** 3g|**Sat Fat:** 0g|**Carbohydrates:** 3g|**Fiber:** 1g|**Sugar:** 3g|**Protein:** 2g

Cheesy Buffalo Sauce

Preparation Time: 5 minutes
Cooking Time: 0 minutes
Servings: 1 cup

Ingredients:

- ½ cup cashews, soaked

- ¼ cup

- 3 tablespoons hot sauce

- 1½ tablespoons nutritional yeast

- Salt to taste

Preparation:

1. Take a blender and add all the ingredients to it.

2. Blend until smooth.

3. Store in an airtight container in the refrigerator and use when required. Consume within 3 weeks.

Serving Suggestion: Serve with yummy hot chicken wings.

Variation Tip: You can add white pepper.

Nutritional Information per Serving:

Calories: 44| **Fat:** 3g|**Sat Fat:** 0g|**Carbohydrates:** 2g|**Fiber:** 0g|**Sugar:** 1g|**Protein:** 2g

Avocado Dip

Preparation Time: 5 minutes
Cooking Time: 0 minutes
Servings: 1 cup

Ingredients:

- 2 avocados
- ½ cup cilantro
- ¼ cup lime juice

Preparation:

1. Add all the ingredients to a blender.

2. Blend until smooth.

3. Store in an airtight container in the refrigerator and use within 3 to 4 days.

Serving Suggestion: Serve it with chicken lettuce wraps.

Variation Tip: You can also add fresh chilies.

Nutritional Information per Serving:

Calories: 42| **Fat:** 4g|**Sat Fat:** 1g|**Carbohydrates:** 3g|**Fiber:** 2g|**Sugar:** 0g|**Protein:** 0g

Chimichurri Sauce

Preparation Time: 5 minutes
Cooking Time: 0 minutes
Servings: 1 cup

Ingredients:

- 1 jalapeno, stems removed
- ½ cup coconut oil
- 1 cup cilantro
- 1 cup parsley
- 1 shallot
- 2 cloves garlic
- 1 tablespoon lime juice
- Salt to taste
- Pepper to taste

Preparation:

1. Take a blender and add all of the ingredients to it.

2. Blend until smooth.

3. Store in an airtight container in the refrigerator and use within 2 weeks.

Serving Suggestion: Serve with chicken or lean beef.

Variation Tip: Avocado oil can be used instead.

Nutritional Information per Serving:

Calories: 126| **Fat:** 14g|**Sat Fat:** 1g|**Carbohydrates:** 2g|**Fiber:** 0.2g|**Sugar:** 0.3g|**Protein:** 0.1g

Buffalo Dill Sauce

Preparation Time: 10 minutes
Cooking Time: 0 minutes
Servings: 1 cup

Ingredients:

- 1 cup mayo
- 1½ teaspoon dill weed
- 2 teaspoon Franks Hot Sauce
- ½ teaspoon pepper
- Salt to taste

Preparation:

1. Take a bowl and add all of the ingredients to it.

2. Mix well and serve.

Serving Suggestion: Serve with hot chicken wings.

Variation Tip: You can add mint leaves for a fresh flavor.

Nutritional Information per Serving:

Calories: 933| **Fat:** 78.8g|**Sat Fat:** 11.5g|**Carbohydrates:** 60g|**Fiber:** 1g|**Sugar:** 15.1g|**Protein:** 3.3g

30 Days Meal Plan

DAY 1

Healthy Eggs Benedict

Potato Pork Salad

Roasted Radish

Chicken Soup

Strawberry Ice Cream

DAY 2

Egg Muffins

Stuffed Sweet Potatoes

Roast Potatoes

Chicken Pie Soup

Chia Coconut Pudding

DAY 3

Sweet Potato Hash

Cauliflower Rice Curry

Roasted Cauliflower

Thai Chicken Coconut Soup

Mango Banana Ice Cream

DAY 4

Pork Breakfast Salad

Thyme Roasted Carrots

Shakshuka Delight

Healthy Toscana Soup

Strawberry Coconut Cream

DAY 5

Banana Smoothie Bowl

Chicken Fajitas

Brussels Sprouts

Tomato Soup

Sweet Fruit Salad0

DAY 6

Zucchini Noodles Breakfast

Parsnip Alfredo

Green Beans with Roasted Almonds

Broccoli Soup

Avocado Ice Cream

DAY 7

Pumpkin and Almond Porridge

Carnitas Delight

Green Beans with Garlic

Buffalo Chicken Chowder

Coconut Chocolate Pudding

DAY 8

Super Quick Breakfast Skillet

Lamb Stew

Roasted Red Cabbage

Chicken Soup

Caramel Apples

DAY 9

Berry Smoothie

Egg Salad

Mash Potatoes

Chicken Pie Soup

Blueberry Delight

DAY 10

Chorizo Omelet

Potato Chili

Cilantro Cauliflower Rice

Thai Chicken Coconut Soup

Avocado Mousse

DAY 11

Moroccan Omelet

Pineapple Chicken

Shakshuka Delight

Healthy Toscana Soup

Avocado Mousse

DAY 12

Waffle Omelet

Asparagus Delight

Brussels Sprouts

Tomato Soup

Blueberry Delight

DAY 13

Spinach Coconut Smoothie

Chicken Wings

Green Beans with Roasted Almonds

Broccoli Soup

Caramel Apples

DAY 14

Pumpkin and Almond Porridge

Chicken Broccoli Stir Fry

Green Beans with Garlic

Buffalo Chicken Chowder

Coconut Chocolate Pudding

DAY 15

Super Quick Breakfast Skillet

Lamb Stew

Roasted Red Cabbage

Chicken Soup

Sweet Fruit Salad

DAY 16

Berry Smoothie

Egg Salad

Mash Potatoes

Cauliflower Rice Curry

Avocado Ice Cream

DAY 17

Sweet Potato Hash

Potato Chili

Cilantro Cauliflower Rice

Ginger Carrot Soup

Chia Coconut Pudding

DAY 18

Moroccan Omelet

Pineapple Chicken

Shakshuka Delight

Stuffed Pepper Soup

Strawberry Coconut Cream

DAY 19

Waffle Omelet

Cauliflower Mash

Brussels Sprouts

Lemon Pepper Salmon

Mango Banana Ice Cream

DAY 20

Spinach Coconut Smoothie

Chicken Salad

Green Beans with Roasted Almonds

Broccoli Salad

Chia Coconut Pudding

DAY 21

Pumpkin and Almond Porridge

Lime Coconut Chicken

Green Beans with Garlic

Roast Beef

Strawberry Ice Cream

DAY 22

Berry Smoothie

Lamb Stew

Roasted Red Cabbage

Chicken Soup

Avocado Mousse

DAY 23

Berry Smoothie

Egg Salad

Mash Potatoes

Brussels Sprouts Chicken Skillet

Caramel Apples

DAY 24

Egg Muffins

Potato Chili

Cilantro Cauliflower Rice

Chicken with Avocado Salad

Strawberry Ice Cream

DAY 25

Moroccan Omelet

Pineapple Chicken

Shakshuka Delight

Roasted Cauliflower

Blueberry Delight

DAY 26

Waffle Omelet

Cauliflower Mash

Brussels Sprouts

Salmon Veg Salad

Sweet Fruit Salad

DAY 27

Spinach Coconut Smoothie

Chicken Salad

Green Beans with Roasted Almonds

Broccoli Salad

Chia Coconut Pudding

DAY 28

Healthy Eggs Benedict

Lime Coconut Chicken

Green Beans with Garlic

Roast Beef

Mango Banana Ice Cream

DAY 29

Spinach Coconut Smoothie

Lamb Stew

Thyme Roasted Carrots

Chicken Soup

Coconut Chocolate Pudding

DAY 30

Zucchini Noodles Breakfast

Potato Chili

Roasted Radish

Lemon Chicken

Avocado Ice Cre

Conclusion

The 30 Days Whole Foods Diet is a healthy and nutritious diet primarily based on whole, unprocessed foods. It restricts certain food categories from your diet, such as legumes, alcohol, grains, dairy products, artificial sweeteners, sugar, and soy products. It is a 30-day long diet that is beneficial in promoting healthy eating habits, improving metabolism, and encouraging weight loss. It is a complete lifestyle and should be adhered to in the long term if you want to continue experiencing its benefits.